Faith's Journey

A Story of Discipleship

Faith's Journey

A Story of Discipleship

by Fr. Doug Lorig

Theosis Press
5121 N. 71st Pl.
Paradise Valley, AZ. 85253

Printed in the United States of America

International Standard Book Number- 978-0-9833257-1-0 (paperback)

Printed and bound by Lulu Publishing

Library of Congress Control Number: 2017944286

Cover Photo - The Mexican Poppy blooms in the desert, as I know my soul has done, so I want to thank my friend Dan Hahne for letting me use his beautiful photo on the cover.

Foreword: Faith's Journey

Dr. Jeffrey P Wincel, D. Min.

It is an honor for me to write a foreword to Fr. Doug Lorig's new book, *Faith's Journey: A Story of Discipleship.* As a parishioner, directee and friend of Fr. Doug, the example of his life's journey taught me much about the path of discipleship. I am confident that reading this book will do the same for you.

The telling of one's life story is always a delicate balance. Sharing the important events and experiences of life, the times of doubt or failure, the revelations and insights given by God, and maintaining humility while doing so is difficult for any of us. For a man like Fr. Doug, this is doubly challenging, as his life has been one of service to God, his family, to his Church, and to his fellow man. Ego, hubris, focus on self is not characteristics that come naturally to him, so telling his own story draws Fr. Doug into uncomfortable waters. Fortunately for us, Fr. Doug shares his story with us.

Traveling through his growth, conversion, and trials, Fr. Doug, shares with us the key mysteries of the Christian faith, as he has experienced them. Both the mystical and practical experiences shared by Fr. Doug illumines a spiritual journey in ways that are both refreshing and unique. They show us a way to Mercy, discovery and love.

Fr Doug's book is especially serious about his relationship to the Blessed Mother, and the mysteries in Christ that She draws us to. The special and unique role that Mary has played in Fr. Doug's life is one that we too can experience. Through his reflection on our Blessed Mother, the mystics and the Saints, Fr Doug points us toward our divine relationship (Theosis) that is possible in the all-encompassing Mystery of the Triune God. Fr. Doug shows us a life in our relationship with Him that is far more than simply external and observed, instead one that is internal and intimate.

Faith's Journey reminds us that we all desire to experience the fullness of God in a way that is nothing less than personal and intimate. In his life story, Fr. Doug shows us that his total, selfless surrender to the draw of the Holy Spirit has become the foundation of his life. He shows us that this really is both the origin and objective of all we desire and only this will ever satisfy our yearning hearts. Fr. Doug invites each of us to embrace and enjoy our own life's journey of faith.

It is my hope that those who read and enjoy this book will want to wade into the deeper waters of the spiritual life. Fr. Doug gives us a wonderful 'taste' of the life of the disciple. As we journey ourselves, we will want to take up his book time and time again to follow his example; and like Fr. Doug, to open ourselves to the possibilities to be in intimate and total communion with our loving God.

Dedication –

My last pastoral assignment was St. Maria Goretti Catholic Church in Scottsdale, Arizona. At 80, and slowed down by Parkinson's Disease, I retired after being their pastor for ten years. It was in this beautiful parish that my priestly life and ministry bloomed. Age and grace! So, I dedicate this little witness to the parishioners and staff of St. Maria's. God bless each one of you for letting me be a real spiritual father to you. May every priest you have in the years to come recognize your sweet soul.

Contents

Contents

Acknowledgements

I want to thank my friend Dr. Jeff Wincel for pushing me to write this little book, and for his very insightful editing. I am deeply indebted to him - and how wonderful that God put him in my parish, a man so steeped in patristic spirituality.

And of course, I want to thank my wife, Nancy, who has walked beside me all these years. In little St. Thomas Byzantine Catholic Church, our parish now that I am retired, she is Pani Nancy, a greeting of respect for a priest's wife. Mnohaja L'ita! God grant you many years!

Chapter 1 - Orientation

"If you are a theologian, you will pray truly. And if you pray truly, you are a theologian."

Evagrius the Solitary
Treatise on Prayer, 61

In the West we see theology as something a person studies, becomes qualified to write and teach, and is then given the title of "theologian". The temptation is to think that once we have given an intellectual ascent to what Jesus has taught us, we have locked it in, having now attained spiritual knowledge. The Orthodox Churches see theology from a much more mystical perspective. To be a theologian, for them, means of course to know the theology of the church, but more specifically to have true spiritual knowledge from actually practicing it - being doers of Christ's commands. This is how the Holy Spirit makes one a theologian.

Well known Orthodox Elder, Sophrony Sakharov, taught that knowledge of God is given to those who actually do what Jesus taught - that if we don't let our theology flower through authentic daily practice of his commandments, we are like a bird with only one wing. The little creature will keep looking up and dreaming of one day flying to the heights, but it will never happen. Experiential knowledge of God comes from doing what Jesus commanded, and never from just talking about it. One could say the devil knows more theology than any of us, but has no spiritual wisdom because he doesn't practice it.

Doers of the Word

Extremely enlightened doers of the word do exist - especially (but not exclusively) in monasteries where the patristic way of unitive spirituality is put into practice. We know of them because their disciples usually write books to share their Spirit-given wisdom with the rest of us. Unitive spirituality centers on starving the passions - which come about because we cave in to some of the 7 deadly sins until they become habitual - and living fully the commandments of Christ, summarized in Matthew 5, 6, and 7. - all of course in the context of a life centered on Prayer and Christ's life-giving sacraments.

The plan of God for our salvation leads us to theosis - to divinization . We become in fact, and not just theoretically sons and daughters of God, sharing by GRACE the intimacy Christ has with the Trinity by NATURE. For us this happens in Heaven. We become "gods" by participation. As the priest says in the silent prayer when he pours a little water into the wine before the consecration, "Through the mystery of this water and wine, MAY WE COME TO SHARE IN THE

DIVINITY OF CHRIST, WHO HUMBLED HIMSELF TO SHARE IN OUR HUMANITY."

This clear reference to theosis mirrors what St. Augustine and later St. Thomas Aquinas said: God became man that man might become god. This can shake up a Catholic who has never heard such language before, knowing that only God can be God! But of course, we would agree - only God can be God. What theosis bestows on us by grace is the adoption of sons and daughters as taught by St. Paul, and does not mean we somehow become part of the essence of God himself. We "participate" in Christ's divine nature as his brothers and sisters - adopted by his Father. When St. John of the Cross experienced this mystical union, he said God treated him like an equal!

Simply put, Jesus was sent to us by the Father through the Holy Spirit and the Blessed Virgin Mary, to become fully human while remaining fully divine. He redeemed us with his own blood and then called us to follow him back to the Father - to the intimate embrace of the Trinity. And that, the Apostle Paul assures us ,no eye has seen, no ear has heard, no mind has conceived (what God has in store for those who love him!).

This "following back" means walking with Jesus, who is the way, by starving the passions (ascetic practice) and keeping his specific commands - which we have said are summarized in Matthew 5,6, and 7. Our sins are symptoms of the passions we ourselves have cultivated. Confession takes care of the sins - the symptoms - but living the Gospel commands Jesus teaches helps chip away at the control particular passions have gained over us if we practice them in the context of prayer, repentance, and the sacraments. The focus on confession is strong in the West, and rightly so, but the equally critical battle against the causes of our sins, with heavy emphasis on keeping Jesus' gospel commandments is not as rich as it is in the East, and particularly in the writings that deal with the patristic teaching on unitive spirituality.

Rediscovering Theosis

In 2016 Pope Francis met with the heads of the many religious orders of our Catholic Church. The meeting, held in Rome, featured a call on the part of the Holy Father, for our religious orders to rediscover theosis! To rediscover theosis, of course, is to rediscover patristic unitive theology and the spirituality that goes with it. Francis was asking them to re-form their orders by placing theosis in a place of honor - I think as the ideal. In doing that he is calling for them to produce holy monks and nuns with experiential knowledge of God, so they can become Spirit-bearing guides for those of us living out our lives in Catholic Churches.

We who struggle to walk in the footsteps of those who have embraced the unitive way need to have experienced guides
who themselves live it every day. In the West we have St. John of the Cross, but there are very few giving spiritual direction in the unitive way. If we do not have an experienced guide, we are constantly in danger of falling into the ditches on either side of the road - especially through pride.

For example, the Pharisees had 613 laws to follow. We have more than 1,700 at last count! If they became legalistic and proud, placing lesser laws above "the weightier matters of the law" such as Mercy (landing in the ditch), we Catholics are even more subject to the same distortion of Christ's way. God resists the proud.

East meets West – Spiritual Direction

So, for steady spiritual direction these past forty years, I have had to look to the Orthodox Spirit-bearing fathers. St. John of the Cross was very disturbed by the lack of the kind of spiritual directors the nuns needed. I have to say I did learn about the primacy of humility and love from St. Therese of Lisieux, who has walked with me on this journey from the very beginning, but the whole world of teaching on love and humility is dominated by the Eastern patristic tradition. So it is the Orthodox holy ones who have kept me on course, and out of the ditches all these years.

God placed me with one foot in the East and one in the West. Is it possible he does not accept the separation of our two great ancient churches? Maybe we have to live with the consequences of what Catholic historians say we both caused, with arrogance on both sides, but God himself is not bound to the decisions made then. He is free to act in any way he wills. St. John Paul II, knowing the richness of the East, calls on us to recognize that richness and "breath from both lungs." That is what I believe the Holy Spirit has asked me to do.

I pray my Latin Church will one day embrace our unitive spirituality, preserved and practiced in the East, and recover what we knew in ancient times. We have watched the last three popes place reunion with the Eastern Churches in a very favored place during their pontificates, with Pope Francis now leading the way with his wonderful expressions of fraternal love and respect for the Orthodox Patriarchs who have visited him in Rome. God grant that soon we can be one again!

Chapter 2 – Before Nancy

God built heaven and earth to be the dwelling place of the human race. But he also built the human body and soul to make them his own abode, so that he might dwell therein and rest there as in a well kept house.... 'We are his house' (Heb 3:6).

Pseudo-Macarius
Forty Ninth Homily

My Irish mother was a Methodist and my German father a Lutheran. When I came along mom wanted her pastor to baptize me - she was very fond of him and my dad didn't offer any resistance. Later, mom joined the Lutheran Church, and that set the course for all of my faith experiences growing up,

Our parish church was only a block away - a very small town block- so maybe a two-minute walk. I have very fond memories of those years, with friends, wonderful adults, and Sunday School classes that I loved. I did NOT love the "angry God" I heard about nearly every Sunday morning in the pastor's homily. Maybe it was just me, but I could not bring myself to love a God who blasts you with threats of doom one minute and then adds, "But you do realize I love you." First a fist, and then a kiss on the cheek. It seemed so disingenuous to me. I think that is why I went on such a determined hunt for the God of love I found in St. John's Gospel - and in the stories of Jesus' gentleness with sinners. It seemed to me his "anger" was pretty much aimed at hypocrites.

Rejoice with those who rejoice

Decades later, after learning about the love of God from St. Therese of Lisieux, I read a Catholic book about St. Isaac of Syria. It was like finding the holy grail! Here is a quote from "The Spiritual World of Isaac The Syrian" by Hilarion Alfeyev, in the Cistercian Study Series of books:

> "In Isaac's understanding God is above all immeasurable and boundless love. The conviction that God is love dominates Isaac's thought: it is the source of his theological opinions, ascetical recommendations, and mystical insights. His theological system cannot be comprehended apart from this fundamental concept. Divine love surpasses human understanding and verbal description. At the same time this love is reflected in God's actions with respect to the created world and humankind: 'Among all his actions there is none which is not entirely a matter of mercy, love, and compassion: this constitutes the beginning and the end of his dealings with us.' Both the creation of the world and God's coming to earth in flesh had as its only aim 'to reveal his boundless love to the world'. Divine love was the main reason why God created the universe and is the main driving force behind the whole of creation."

What I knew from childhood - by a blessed intuition - I now saw reflected in St. Isaac's teaching. Therese from the West and Isaac from the East are, I am sure, next door neighbors in the divine mansions Jesus prepared for them!

I went off to a Lutheran high school for grades 10-12. It was a good school with wonderful teachers. For me, it was very trying because my neurology doesn't include the ability to memorize, and most all of the classes required a great deal of it. I suffered when my name was called and I had to stammer and look down at my feet because I couldn't remember what I now had to recite. Only in college did that change when I took some courses that did not require memorizing, but did require a lot of reflection and theory. I suddenly started getting higher grades, and was not on the bottom of the class. I remember how good that felt. I still can't memorize, and as well as I know the Mass, I have to mostly read it when I celebrate.

Since the school was about an hour and a half north of our home, I stayed at the school dorm most weekends. For fun, I would take the Selby-Lake bus and get off at St. Paul Cathedral. Built by a very powerful Archbishop named John Ireland, I loved to light a candle or two at every altar. In a semicircle behind the main altar the Archbishop put many altars, with saints from the European countries his parishioners had left to come to America. I didn't know I was supposed to pay for them, so the candle fund probably recorded a little loss for those three years!

I would begin on the right side at the Sacred Heart altar, and light my way around to the Mary altar on the far left. I spent most of my time there. She always seemed to be drawing me to connect with her in prayer. I found rosaries on the pews, but didn't know how to pray them. Of course, now I can understand all of that quiet calling a lot better than I did then.

After praying in the cathedral, I would walk down the hill to the German Church of the Assumption and pray there for a while. Then I would get a burger and Coke at Mickey's Dinner which was near Assumption church and then head back to the dorm.

Weep with those who weep

It is interesting that Archbishop Ireland was one of the loudest voices against immigrants from Eastern Europe (Byzantine Catholics) bringing their married priests with them to serve them in their American communities. In 1930 (after Archbishop's death) Rome did forbid this practice and half a million Byzantine Catholics are said to have left the Church, being so scandalized, and went to Russian Orthodox Churches.

Now, at 16, I am sitting in the Mary chapel of the cathedral Archbishop Ireland built, thinking about being a Catholic - and would one day do that, as a married priest - and one who wanted to be Byzantine! Even more interesting, I would one day concelebrate Mass at the cathedral with one of Archbishop's successor, and vest a new priest for that Diocese. Also, the new priest's first Mass was at Assumption - the German church I always visited. He had asked me to preach the homily there at his first Mass. Was Archbishop rolling over in his grave, or was he one of my intercessors - trying to mend a sin against love with regard to the Byzantines?

After some college, I went to Lutheran seminary but did not complete my final year. Instead I finished my degree in Social Work and practiced that profession in three public schools in a very poor county. It was then that I met Nancy, my soul mate, studied for Episcopal priesthood, was ordained, and served first as a deacon in a small mission and later as priest in a larger church. My parents had no problem with that because it was not Catholic....in those days, there was shame if someone from your German Lutheran family joined the Catholic Church.

Such is the sign of purity

Nancy was also raised Lutheran, but followed me into the Episcopal Church and later all the way to Catholic. I suppose it was easier on my mom and dad that I became Catholic an inch at a time, but when it did happen, it took them ten years to accept it and attend my Masses when they visited us. The Episcopal Church was wonderful, but in the end, it could not give me what I needed. Mary kept "whispering" in my heart that I needed to come home. My dad's family were all Catholics - from Germany. My grandfather left the Catholic Church to marry my grandmother, who was Lutheran and the prettiest girl in town! Even in her 80's she was still beautiful. Home, I came later to understand, was the Catholic Church, and it seems now like all of heaven was conspiring to get us there!

Chapter 3 - Arizona

"True commitment, my friend comes from only one source: the love of God. It is indeed that very love that shows itself in all the many facets of our human existence. It is this love that allows itself through the action of the Holy Spirit, to move us to loving activity consistently, generously, and eagerly. This is the expression of true Christian commitment"

St. Francis de Sales
Introduction to the Devout Life

A Journey of Faith

After having served my Episcopal parish in Minnesota for three years, I began to feel very strongly that my next parish was waiting for me in Colorado or Arizona, but I had no idea which. I was afraid this new "calling" may simply be all just a mess in my head instead of God's grace - all the more unsettling because Nancy was about to deliver twins Amy and Heather, and our son Michael was just two years old. I wondered how irresponsible was I being by even entertaining the notion I was being called somewhere else?

I asked my best friend to drive to Denver with me so I could see the Bishop of Colorado. He said yes, and we headed West while our families waited at home. We arrived in Denver, and before going to sleep we knelt between the beds and prayed for guidance. It was a powerful moment in the quietest sort of way. In my prayer I knew, without knowing how or why, that the parish God would be sending me to serve would have very distinct markers.

First, it would have a leaky roof. It wasn't, I understood, just a small leak, but a massive issue for the parish. Second, the parish was very close to an area of serious poverty. Third, there were only a handful of parishioners because of infighting. Finally, there were three couples praying for God to please send them a priest. At this point I really felt that I was losing it - making all of this up in my head. But my friend said I had to trust God.

The next day I called the Diocese of Colorado to see if I could get an appointment with the Bishop. I was told that the Bishop was attending a conference for several days and wouldn't be available. They did give me his phone number so I could talk to him between sessions. He must have taken a little break because my call went through on the first try, and he began telling me of two parishes I could contact because they were looking for pastors. I asked him if either one had a leaky roof. He laughed and said no - both were very well maintained. I thanked him and we drove back to Minnesota with the conviction that my work was to be found in Arizona.

Family Matters

When the twins were two weeks old, the doctor released us for travel. Amy and Heather in baskets, Michael in the front seat between us, and pulling a twenty-four-foot travel trailer, we headed south in the dead of winter. As we pulled out, I felt totally out of my right mind on the one hand, and at great peace on the other. If my rational, German, well ordered wife had not agreed with me I would have stayed put, but she was determined to take this journey with me, and in spite of very practical concerns, we drove away. We got as far as Osceola, Iowa before a blinding snowstorm stopped us. The heater in the trailer refused to ignite, so that meant a motel. I was paralyzed by the thought that I had been irresponsible and now we are stopped and don't have money enough to get to Arizona if we have to pay for several days in a motel. I kept thinking, what have I done?

Nancy calmly took care of the motel and informed me that a parishioner had told her I was too stupid to plan where money is concerned, and that we would be needing some - and with that gave her a thousand dollars. She told Nancy not to tell me until the money was needed. Grandma Ruth, as the girls and Michael called her a few years later when she visited us in Arizona, was our angel for a very scary time, and that kind of provision kept happening at times when someone's help was needed to get us from one work to another - that continued even after our conversion to Catholicism.

Finally, we arrived in Tucson. Happy to be warmer and at our destination, we set up in a trailer park and began to think about how to approach the Bishop of Arizona. It was the end of the week, so looking in a directory we found Grace Episcopal Church and decided to attend Sunday Eucharist there. Maybe the rector would know if there were any parishes available.

Before services began I went to the sacristy and asked the pastor about parish vacancies. He said there were two the last he heard, but one of them was a terrible place and the parishioners ate priests for breakfast! He warned me not to apply there. Actually, that sounded like the place that fit the four markers.

Sitting in the back of the church with my family and no clerical garb, a woman walked in and then looking at me as she passed our pew asked me if I was a priest. I have no idea how she knew. I said yes and she told me she was the Bishop's wife. I told her about the conversation with the rector and she said I should talk to her husband. So, after the liturgy I did talk with him. Providence had put us in the very church he was visiting that day. He told me to call Sierra Vista and Nogales. Both were looking for pastors, although the Bishop's Committee had just recommended they close down Nogales - for pretty obvious reasons. He voiced reservations about that decision and said I should call them anyway.

The next day I did call Sierra Vista, and they already had a candidate and were informing the Bishop so they could get his approval. That left Nogales - a border town with a Nogales, Sonora just across the line. I called, but there was no answer. Finally, after multiple attempts we decided to drive there.

Nogales Arizona?

When we arrived, we found the church just north of town - stark modern, no cross, the property overgrown with tumbleweed and grasses. It looked abandon. I rang the doorbell at the rectory but no one answered. All of the buildings were attached - church, hall in the middle, rectory on the right. It was in a subdivision built around a country club, but it looked like the project had not really grown as planned.

Not finding anyone at the rectory we drove to some nearby houses and I knocked on the door of one of them. A woman answered and I asked her if she knew who was the Senior Warden of St. Andrew. She asked if I was a priest and when I told her I was she said they needed me a whole lot more than I needed them! Well, once again this sounded like the sad parish with the four markers. She gave me his number and let me use her phone to set up a meeting - in ten minutes he would arrive.

When we got back to the church we only waited a few minutes and the Senior Warden did arrive. He went inside and brought out some folding chairs for us. He said there was no heat and it would be warmer out in the sun. My first question was whether or not the roof leaked. He looked stunned and then asked how I knew. He said it was really bad, was going to cost thousands of dollars the parish did not have, and that everyone was very demoralized over it. He said they had a very sophisticated furnace but could not afford to use it. The air conditioning was useless because they could not afford to put in the transformer required to run it. All very depressing for them.

I asked why the money wasn't there and he said they only had about 30 active families left because of some really ugly disagreements. Two markers down and two to go. Across the border, a short distance away, there were hills and shacks - with a lot of very poor people. Marker number three. I agreed to officiate at services for the next several weeks, which included Christmas. When I asked the Senior Warden why he accepted me so readily he said he and his wife and two other couples had been praying together for a priest to come to St. Andrew. The fourth marker! Just a few days before we arrived, a priest from Pennsylvania who was considering coming called and said he could not accept their offer. Then he said they should keep praying because he felt God was going to send a priest. Actually he told them God would send them a priest right down the chimney for Christmas!

We took the invitation to celebrate the Sunday Eucharist at St. Andrew for two weekends and then Christmas - after which they called me officially and the Bishop gave his approval. That was forty years ago. One of the priests told me they had had twenty-five priests in seventy-five years - and had a reputation for treating them very badly.

The Greatest Commandment

The very first Sunday after being made their pastor I put up two cutouts I had made the day before with plywood and a saber saw. The first said, "This is my Commandment", and the other said, "That you love one another". I put one on each wall beside the altar. The homily was on this verse, and at the end of it I asked that anyone willing to walk with me in this Commandment should stand. The whole congregation stood, and we were off and running. I served them four years, and insisted on love as the only future they had. After I left, the next priests stayed much longer. What God wanted wasn't just to fill an empty slot in one of his churches - he wanted it to be healed - and I can tell you it was love alone that finally turned them around.

Love grew as I made it the theme of all of my pastoral teaching. In time God gave them a real opportunity to love their neighbors in the form of a free clinic for crippled Mexican children. It only took place one day a month, but they were now thinking of others. Some resisted my determination to give the free clinic space in the hall, but it was a resistance now tempered by love. They did agree that the hall sat empty all week, every week.

I had not gone looking for something we might do in that hall. Two Catholic women had stopped by and said that doctors from Tucson came monthly to treat crippled children from Mexico to give their medical students experience with polio and club foot because they were more common in Mexico. In addition, it was a veritable workshop for prosthetic devices training. They wanted to move the free clinic to the American side of the border for easier passage of the doctors. The local Catholic parish did not have space available so they decided to ask us.

Divine Providence strikes again! I said yes, absolutely, and today, close to forty years later, that clinic is alive and well and serves far more children than it did in my day. The parish still cooks for the

Mexican parents and families who bring the kids to the hall, and this once a month event is now part of the DNA of St. Andrew. Love found a home at that once divided parish, and not only healed some very open wounds, but gave the parish a future. Why do we have such a hard time realizing what Swiss Theologian Hans Urs Von Balthazar, Jesuit thinker Teilhard De Chardin, and so many others have taught - that love alone unites?

Healing of the Spirits

The probable cause of so much division when they were located downtown was, I think, a mix of very independent people - Southwesterners - and on the new site, a really big problem. When the state put in a freeway exit for downtown Nogales, it ran right through their little jewel of a church. The pastor moved them to a new country club area with dreams of lots of new parishioners, which did not materialize, and built an ultramodern structure the parishoners called a barn. There was no cross to identify it as a church - all very distressing in light of their beautiful little traditional church downtown. To make matters worse, it was built over an Indian cemetery and there were constant episodes that justified the claim that it was haunted. Of course, no one told me about any of this. But the very first night in the rectory we found out!

The rectory had no furniture, so we moved the couch/bed from the trailer into the bedroom. The girls had their baskets and Michael slept on some pillows. Before bed, Nancy was working in the kitchen and when she looked down the hall toward our room she saw an Indian, fierce and menacing. Then he disappeared.

She never saw such things before. She didn't say anything to me about it, so I had no idea there was anything wrong until the middle of the night when I was awakened by a figure bending over me. I yelled and sat right up - shaking from the encounter.

The next day I walked around in the church, praying in the chapel and generally snooping in the sacristy to see what I had to work with. I was very aware of someone following me around, but there was no one to see. It got really spooky in the chapel because pews from the old church were in there - on the concrete floor - and when I sat down, a pew across the aisle squeaked as though someone just sat down on it. I stood, walked around a bit and coming back into the chapel I sat down again and the pew across the aisle squeaked. I had enough of this, and went back to the rectory to call the young man who was their pastor before me. He told me the construction crew dug into a cemetery of Las Trincheras Indians and had desecrated it by plowing bones and artifacts under, taking artifacts, and generally made no attempt to respect those buried there. That is when the "haunting" episodes began. He said the old man who was following me around was harmless and that his wife "saw" him all the time.

My first response was to offer prayer for the souls of those buried there, and I did that again and again. It was a little better, but still not settled. Then, as we hand dug a small dry well for the sacrarium in the sacristy - just outside the sacristy door - we found cremations- in pots, buried a foot or so below the surface. As soon as we uncovered a few of them, I told them to stop digging and went to the rectory to call the University of Arizona in Tucson. This had to be done correctly, and respectfully.

Just an aside here - neither Nancy nor I had ever had such experiences. Blessing places with odd happenings, yes, but this was much more. I discerned that we were dealing with human souls, so that helped us pray as well. This was really the beginning of my own priestly concern for the dead, which God fortified later - actually in a large way - and I have now been praying for them for 40 years.

The University came a few days later. The night before they came I had a strange dream\vision - not sure which - where an old man was walking around on the hill, bent over, and carrying a young girl. She was dead, and her head, legs and arms were limp. He appeared to be in mourning, maybe wanting me to know how terrible this was. I felt the girl was very young, and the man was old, and that made me think it was his granddaughter. Las Trincheras Indians came up from Mexico and were planters, peaceful people. They occupied this site about a thousand years ago, and of course buried their dead - some were full inhumations and some cremations.

When the team from U of A arrived, they questioned me about the find, and then asked if there were any paranormal events associated with uncovering the pots. That was interesting! I told them the history, and then about my vision\dream the night before. Then they took the pots off to their lab in Tucson. Sometime later they returned. The pots were cleaned and the cremains - which had bone pieces - were in little paper bags inside their respective pots. The pots were rough and primitive, but one was red and decorated - very elegant. The team said it was probably the cremains of a very important person in the tribe and the pot was probably gotten through trade with other Indians. Then one of them reminded me of the old man and the girl. "I don't want to lead you on, but the largest pot had a smaller pot inside it. The cremains in the large pot were of an old man, and the cremains in the small pot were those of a young girl. I immediately wondered if this was that old man who gently followed me around whenever I was at the church - just as he had the previous pastor's wife.

We built a little "tomb" in the hallway just outside the sanctuary so the remains of these people would have a respectful place until we figured out where they belonged. Sometime after we made the little place for them, an Indian came to see me about a wedding. He and his wife had divorced and now wanted to remarry. We got to talking and I told him the whole story. He said the fierce one was probably a medicine man who was guarding the graves. He said the Indians believed they had two souls, one goes to God when they die, and the other remains at their grave. He said the souls knew I was respectful and that maybe I could help bring some peace to that hill. Of course this is all very different from our Catholic view, but lacking any wisdom on this I decided to keep praying for these souls to find peace. My Indian friend painted a picture of the old man sitting on our hill and looking off into the distance. We hung it above the little tomb. In time the cremains, I understand, were given over to the Indian community for proper burial - after we left Nogales.

Places are sometimes in need of healing. Wounds somehow create land memories - wounds that need to be healed. I don't know much about all of these things, but I do know the little said in Scripture is not enough to help understand the mystery of all life after death. We know what God wants us to know, but it is clear that much more exists there than we can see. One thing I do know is that demons never create peace in a place. Liars and deceivers, the false peace they can project just doesn't smell right. Peace did come to that hill when we were kind, loving, and respectful of the people whose remains were buried there. Love united us to them, and in some way we don't understand, healed a piece of land with a very disturbing history.

Chapter 4 – Nine Days

"If the work of our sanctification seems such a hard and impossible task, it is because we do not have the right idea of what it truly is. In truth, holiness consists of one single thing: faithfulness to the will of God."

Jean-Pierre De Caussade
Abandonment to Divine Providence

Pride or Pastoral Care

Writing about the most important event of my life should be easy, but it is not. I am torn between laying it all out in detail, because I believe that is what I am supposed to do as a clear witness to our Latin Church - and keeping it close to my vest as something that can feed pride's proclivity for wounding the soul - often disguised as something good and beneficial. For years, friends have pressed me to write the account of God's graces in my life, because it would inspire others to desire a more serious walk with Christ. And for years I have resisted, fearing what my own pride would do with it. This tension was sometimes relieved a bit because I do tell many of the stories when I teach and preach - they are the best illustrations I have of so many spiritual truths.

I believe God has taught me so much through these events that telling them in the context of instruction is truly a gift I can share with others in my priestly life and work. It was Pope Francis' talk with the heads of religious orders in 2016, telling them they should study and recover theosis that convinced me I need to tell everything, just as it all happened. My whole life, as a man and as a priest revolves around the nine days of theosis I experienced in 1978. So, forgive me for opening up what is ordinarily best kept in the heart alone - and pray for me, that God will not have set me on this ancient path in vain.

Thirsting for God

While still in my Episcopal parish in Minnesota, I began to have a strong desire to experience God himself - not just words about him. I began to read my Bible with a real hunger for his words, and for him. This grace was more like an obsession, which woke me in the middle of the night and took me to my desk to read the gospels over and over - and really the whole of the scriptures.

I took notes, and kept begging God to show up and talk to me. I wanted relationship. I would like to say this only acted when I was idle, but it was 24 - 7. When we arrived in Nogales, Arizona and moved into the rectory of St. Andrew Episcopal Church, this spiritual hunger for relationship with God continued unabated.

Along with this hunger there was a "depression" that wasn't depression as we understand it, but a profound sense of being abandoned - alone - suspended between heaven and earth, and not belonging to either. When I had to minister in any of the many ways priests do that, this lifted, and I was fine, but the moment I finished, the "darkness" was back. Of course, being raised and formed in evangelical protestantism, I had no way of understanding this "refiner's fire", and seeing it as beneficial. All I could do is cry out to God and beg him to take it away.

The Dark Night

I was Pastor of that Nogales parish for 4 years, and the events I will try to relate now did not happen until six months before we left for Phoenix and the Catholic Church. The darkness had started in Minnesota and had been with me for two years, so it was nearly six years before the nine days happened. I would get so desperate I would go to the church at night and bang my fists on the altar and sob and carry on, telling God, who I knew was stoking this refiner's fire, that he had picked the wrong man for this and that I just could not take any more. One of those nights, I heard the kindest voice in my ear, kind but firm, "Doug, it is essential that you endure." From that time on I would still get to that edge of despair but I would stiffen my back and say, " I choose God, no matter what." It kept me from giving up.

Well, without any warning, out of the blue, events began to unfold like a beautifully written play. Wasn't it the Bard who said, "If this were played upon a stage now I could condemn it as an improbable fiction." I had been asked to be one of the ministering priests at a healing service in a Phoenix church. I took my young son along, to relieve Nancy, who had the care of the twins, and we drove to Phoenix. It was a Sunday afternoon in January 1978. It turned out my son was not going to be ok with my leaving him in the pews, so I did not minister. He and I sat and watched as people went to the front for healing prayers. I was wrapped in a great sadness because God would not come and sit with me and talk with me - my relationship obsession. I cried (hiding it from my son) and told God I had reached my limit and would surely crash if he did not do something. I remember saying, "Lord, you absolutely have to do something - I cannot take this anymore. By "something", of course, I meant relationship.

The Morning Star

All the way back to Nogales I felt peace - something that had alluded me for a long time. I was sure it meant he had heard me. But nothing happened. Monday passed, Tuesday, nothing. Then, when I went to bed on the evening of February 1st, I heard music in my head. Not in my whole life had that ever happened. It was from Handel's "Messiah,"…. "The Lord whom you seek will suddenly come to his temple, but who may abide the day of his coming, for he is like a refiner's fire, and like a fuller's soap, and he will refine the sons of Levi (priests) so they will offer their offering in righteousness." I woke up multiple times during the night, and there was that text, taken from the Prophet Malachi. What could this mean? The next morning, February 2nd I went over to the church to set the Altar Book to that date, and found it was the Feast of The Presentation of Christ in the Temple, and the Introit was those words from Malachi I had been hearing all night. I was so excited! I am a priest, and my heart is to be a temple for God, and he is coming! I should have paid more attention to the rest of the reading - the refiner's fire part - I had been experiencing it for years, but in great theological ignorance.

Nothing happened on the 2nd, and nothing on the 3rd, and not until I had given up hope that there would ever be a visit did it finally happen. It was February 14th, Love Day, and I woke up early in the morning to get ready to celebrate the weekday Eucharist. The first thing I was aware of was the silence - not just a lack of noise, but silence in my deepest center. Not the usual rush of thoughts and noise and temptations, but a deep, sacred silence in both my head and my heart. That lasted the entire nine days.

Love is patient

The second gift was love, penetrating and rich and taking over. Really, I thought I could not contain it at all. And if I entered it even a little, it swelled, and was so much I had to ask God to stop or I thought I would explode. It is hard to describe, but both peace and love were not a thing, but a person - or rather a Trinity of persons. Our little twins, Amy and Heather came into the bathroom where I was shaving, and my heart swelled with love so completely that I sat on the floor and played with them - never mind the shaving cream and the celebration of Eucharist in a little while. The love being poured into me overflowed onto our girls, and later it was the same when our son and Nancy woke up. That morning Nancy asked me what was going on - the house and really the whole property was filled with peace. I told her, but what could I say other than it was God? I had no idea of theosis, or the theology around it. All I had was my six year cry for him to show up and talk to me. I was so ignorant.

The nine days that were overflowing with silence and love and peace - which never left, day and night - were filled with other experiences. It was as though Jesus let me experience his virtues and wisdom - communicating to me His very self. I knew this was happening, but had no idea how to explain it to myself other than it being the answer to my six-year quest.

There were only two temptations in the entire nine days. My mind is rarely quiet, and temptations are often and nagging, yet during this time when the Holy Spirit was so present in my soul, only two happened. The first was about halfway through. Completely without warning a really lewd suggestion entered my mind. It was such a contradiction to what I was experiencing that I laughed out loud and said - toward the glass doors where this suggestion seemed to be coming from, "You have got to be kidding!" It, whatever it was, slinked away at being discovered.

The second temptation came like the first, but on the ninth day. It was a temptation to criticize a brother. Just a quick thought is all it was, but revealing! Later that day the whole wonderful event began to fade until it was gone completely. As it faded, I said to the Lord, "Don't come back until my pride has been dealt with." After I said it, prompted I am sure by the Holy Spirit, I suddenly realized that it was my pride that prevented him from staying - my heart was going to have to be healed of a great sickness, pride being the mother of all of it.

During the nine days I could not ask God for a single thing. In fact, I had a list ready should He ever "sit down and talk with me". I had EVERYTHING during those few days - I lacked absolutely nothing because he filled all of the empty spaces in my life. I felt whole for the first time in my life - even noble. Knowing the lightyears that separate me as I am from me as God intended me to be - his image - I could not imagine how he could come at all, let alone remain for all those days.

The Cloud of Unknowing

That evening of the ninth day, I was again feeling the refiner's fire, suspended between heaven and earth, so I went down to the church to beg God to come back. It was awful. I sobbed, I accused Him of making me whole and then throwing me back into my miserable state again. But of course, He just listened and kept on loving me - at a distance.

When I went to bed that night, I asked Him if he could at least tell me what this was. In that moment, in my heart, I saw a dove descend over a pool of water. It was the Holy Spirit and the waters of baptism. Of course I did not understand then, but later learned that theosis is the working out and goal of our baptism. Transfiguration - participation in the divine life as an adopted child of our heavenly Father - right there beside Jesus. It all made my head spin and I began a search to understand what had just happened to me. I knew St. John of the Cross had had some experiences, but I had not read about them. I did read a few days later, but it was all too difficult for me to grasp much, his words being poetry, and in the language of the Scholastics. But I did understand it was union with God and that it was like what had happened to me.

The Desert Fathers

It was my custom to get out of town on my day off, so a few weeks later I drove to St. David, Arizona where the Benedictines have a community. I walked to their little chapel, about the size of a single garage at that time, and sat to pray. On a small table next to the chair was a blue book with excerpts from the Philokalia. Of course I knew nothing of the Philokalia, but as I read my soul just lit up! Here were some answers. I ordered the book, and that was how I got connected to the patristic tradition of the Orthodox Church - the tradition that is also ours, but no longer much more than a few pages in our Latin Seminary courses on patristics. Why was God taking me to this spirituality - not Orthodox, not a monk, married, not even Catholic yet?

One foot in the West and the other in the East. Why? In time I began to understand more and more. The greatest help was to come when I discovered St. Silouan the Athonite in a book by his disciple, Archimandrite Sophrony. Then, some time later I read "His Life Is Mine" by Sophrony. Eventually I discovered Archimandrite Zacharias, Sophrony's disciple and began to devour his books. EVERYTHING was in those books, the whole journey I have been living, and struggling to understand. But even more importantly, Zacharias' books were the best spiritual director I could ever find - and I had at last given up ever finding. But the Philokalia and so many books by and about those who had lived the spirituality I was literally thrust into, had become my spiritual directors, and I knew with absolutely no doubts whatsoever that it was the Mother of God who was arranging everything.

My entire life as a Catholic priest has had as its battery the nine days of grace I experienced in February of 1978. The East - West mystery got even more interesting when I learned that the 14th of February, besides being Valentine's Day and all about love, it is the Feast of St. Cyril and St. Methodius, patrons of Eastern Churches, and the 22nd, when the nine days ended is the Feast of the Chair of Peter. One foot in the East and one in the West. The choice between converting from Episcopal to Catholic or Episcopal to Orthodox had to be made. Nancy agreed, and that is what I would like to tell you about next.

Chapter 5 – Orthodox or Catholic

"While some people seem to have more of an affinity for the spiritual experience than most of us and a very few are mystics, none of us are utterly untouched by this awareness. We are capable of recognizing what the mystics refer to because our own experience is also structured by a horizon of mystery."

David Walsh
Guarded by Mystery

Searching for Home

After nearly four years as Rector of my Episcopal parish in Nogales, Arizona, I was having conversations with my wife Nancy about becoming Catholic. The Eucharist and the Blessed Virgin Mary were now my main areas of study, and I felt very drawn by both for our possible conversion. The problem was that I really liked what I had seen of both the Orthodox and the Catholic respect for the Virgin and for the Real Presence of Christ in their Mass / Divine Liturgy. But which one was home?

I was drawn more to the Orthodox, so that is where I started. It began simply enough with my calling an Orthodox church in Phoenix and asking for prayers to help me quit smoking. Very practical! The priest I spoke with said that he certainly would pray for me, and I thought that was the last of it. A few days later, while picking up after a morning Liturgy on a weekday, three men came into the church, bowed toward the front, crossed themselves, and then approached me. They were Orthodox priests! One, a Greek, was the priest I had called for prayers. He had brought along two other priests, a Greek and an Antiochean. The Greek from Phoenix broke the ice by pointing to the beautiful antique stained-glass windows in my church (of saints, and from the old church) and saying, "Ah, the Episcopalians, they kicked the saints out of the doors in the reformation, but they came back in through the windows!"

After introductions, they said they were going across the line to Nogales, Sonora to have lunch at La Caverna - a popular restaurant in a cave once used as a Mexican jail - and asked if I wanted to go along. I did, and over turtle soup we talked about Orthodoxy and my dilemma. The young Antiochean asked me if I was going to "try for perfection".... a great question. The other two priests shushed him for bringing up something too advanced for me, a newbie. And I really was so ignorant, as I said.

After that day I felt very comfortable with my new Orthodox friends and visited one of them at his church in Tucson. What a good and kind man he was, and so excited about a place called Mt. Athos. He showed me a book with beautiful photos of the monasteries there, and we talked for quite a while. He asked if I wanted to see what his Bishop might say if we were to ask him about me. I said yes, so he called - Chicago I think - after warning me the Bishop could be a bit gruff and sound like he was putting me off.

That turned out to be the case, and when the Bishop asked him if I speak Greek, he more or less barked, "Give him to the Antiocheans." That was it, and the Bishop hung up. Of course, I now realized language and ethnicity were key elements in Orthodox communities, which I should have known, and feeling like an outsider I went back to Nogales. I cannot memorize, so learning a new language, culture and the rest - I was uneasy about such a big step. Nancy felt it would be very hard for our family to fit in. With that, I decided Rome was a choice we could live with as a family, especially since the Byzantine Churches within the Catholic family of Churches had Eastern Liturgy and practice - and married priests until 1930. Rome it would be!

The next question was how to connect with the Roman Catholic Diocese of Phoenix. That was settled when some friends asked us to house-sit in a nice Valley home with a pool! So, knowing the kids would love that, we agreed. While there, we visited a Byzantine Catholic Church in Phoenix. Helping the pastor was an elderly married priest who was in the last class of priests allowed to have a wife, and she was there as well. It was Eastern, Catholic, and very easy to fit in because everyone was used to a priest having a wife. The pastor suggested we call the Diocese of Phoenix and ask if any teaching jobs were still open. It was the end of July and school was to start the third week of August. We did call and yes, St. Mark, an inner city parish had two openings.

Nancy warned me that the Catholic Church would not let me be a priest, but I knew in my heart the Blessed Virgin would never take me this far and then let me down. I assured her, without any evidence at all, that I would be a Catholic priest. The next day we drove to the parish and as we walked through a gate that was between the church and the school, a nun came out the back door of the church. She stopped, looked right at us and said "Are you teachers?" We said yes - Nancy being a teacher and me having a degree so I could teach in Arizona. Without hesitation, she immediately said, "You are hired!" Now normally, no nun would ever say that – there are papers to check, background vetting to be completed, the whole nine yards. So looking shocked, I asked about this sudden answer. She said she had been in the church praying for two teachers - in desperation because school was to start for the teachers in a week. She comes out and there we were!

We taught for that wonderful woman for four years. When she died at the Mother House in Illinois many years later, I flew back to celebrate her funeral Mass, as she had requested in her Will. She was our advocate from that first day at the school in Phoenix until I was ordained to the priesthood in the Catholic Church 5 years later. My first Mass was in the convent where she lived with other IBVM teaching Sisters. God had people in place to help us every step of the way.

The next problem was how to approach the Bishop of Phoenix. I had no case to present that could possibly get him to ordain a married man - as a deacon, yes, but as a priest? Impossible. The answer to this impossible dilemma came in an unexpected way when not many days into the first days of school, all of the Catholic schools in our area were to assemble their students at St. Mary's Basilica in Phoenix for Mass with the Bishop. We bussed our kids and faculty to the church and poured into our places. I remember that I had my class at the very back of the church, on the left side as you enter. When the Bishop came in he was smiling and greeting children as he headed up the aisle. He greeted my class and then looked over them at me - and stared - and paused. Then he walked on, but once on the altar looked back at me and stared again two or three times during the Mass. I was so shaken by this - why was he staring? I was not wearing a clerical collar or anything that suggested I was a priest. When Mass was over I left the class with an aid and ducked out the door before someone from the Diocesan Schools office was to speak. I needed a few minutes to calm down with a cigarette. Suddenly the door burst open and out came the Bishop with his vestments over his arm. He pointed at me and said, "The Holy Spirit told me you are a priest, and I am going to take care of you. Come and see me." He went off to his work and I just stood there stunned.

I did go see the Bishop, and he told me the most amazing thing. He said he could ordain me to the deaconate soon, and eventually could ordain me to the priesthood! I heard him say all of this with a huge sigh of relief, and at the same time, I thought, "I knew Mary would work this out." I couldn't wait to tell Nancy!

The Bishop was the Secretary of the National Conference of Catholic Bishops. Some Episcopal priests had petitioned Paul VI and then John Paul II for Episcopal priests, married or not married, to be ordained as Catholic priests if they converted. The answer was yes - provided the NCCB voted yes in two successive May meetings. One May meeting had resulted in a majority yes vote, and now the 2nd vote would be the next May. He said some of the Bishops were not happy with the majority yes vote and had gone to Rome to lobby against the whole idea - which made the rest of the Bishops upset with them for "going out of house." That, he said, pretty much guaranteed a second majority yes vote in May. And that is how it turned out.

I was ordained deacon in the Catholic Church in July of 1980.

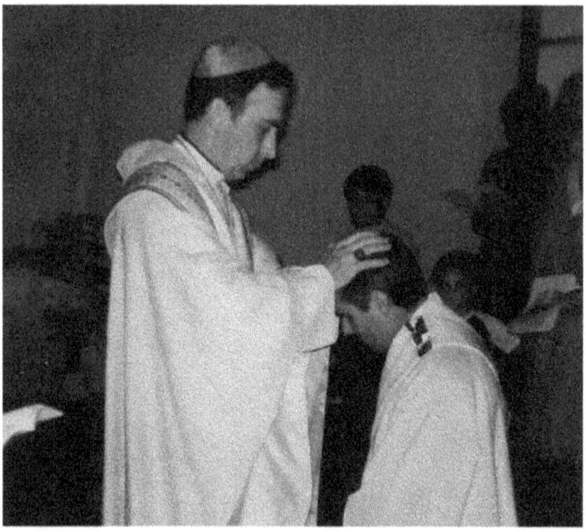

Still having a great love for the spirituality of the East, I asked if I could be ordained for the Byzantine Catholic Church. The Bishop said no because the Byzantine Eparchs had walked out of the Conference when the decision was taken to ordained married men. They had been stripped of their right to ordain married men in 1930 and now the Latins were doing for themselves what they had forbidden them to do - a right they were guaranteed when they had joined Rome hundreds of years ago. So, the Eastern door was closed. I then asked if he would let me be assigned as a bi-ritual deacon to the Byzantine parish we had been attending in Phoenix. He said yes, and I served that parish for nearly five years as I waited for ordination to the priesthood. Ordained a priest June 15, 1984, a Friday - celebrated my first Mass at the convent on Saturday, and my first Divine Liturgy at St, Stephen Byzantine on Sunday.

From Pastor to Priest

The process for preparing ordination was long - 5 years. Vetting, study, examinations, documents - all bundled to be sent off to Rome for the signature of Cardinal Ratzinger, who was then the Prefect of the Congregation for Doctrine of the Faith. After all the years in this process, a huge pause declared by my new Bishop threatened to end everything. The Bishop who had brought me into the Church died suddenly, and a new Bishop was put in his place. Not so sure he wanted to get involved in this whole thing, he called me and said my papers were all ready to send to Rome, but he was unsure about calling for my ordination so he was putting my papers in his bottom drawer for one year! My heart sank. I did not argue, and thanked him for the call. All I could think of was Abraham and Isaac - that had ended well, even though for a time it looked like all the promises would never materialize. Of course, it was all I could think about.

A couple of weeks after the call I accompanied a young Byzantine Catholic priest to Mexico City to visit the Virgin of Guadalupe at her Temple there. He had really serious health issues and wanted to ask her help. He paid my way because he needed someone to help him - Mexico City was not too handicap friendly. When we entered the Basilica, he went off to the Eucharistic Chapel to pray and I went down the aisle to the front where I could see her image better. It was my first time there. When I sat down, I started sobing - from really deep inside - and told her about the Bishop, my papers and the bottom drawer. I promised her solemnly I would work for her the rest of my life if she would get me ordained! That was June 15th, 1983.

In April of 1984 Bishop called me again. I was so afraid he was going to say the decision had been taken not to ordain me. But no, he was calling to say my papers had come back from Rome, signed by Cardinal Ratzinger, and the ordination was on! Since the papers of other men in this process took about a year to process in Rome, this meant Bishop had changed his mind and had sent them on. Mary! To make it an ironclad certainty she helped me, Bishop said the only date open on his calendar was June 15th, 1984! A year to the day. Well, it looks like I will be working for the Virgin Mary for the rest of my life. That is the next thing I want to tell you about.

Chapter 6 – I Work for the Virgin Mary

"Actually, we must stand faithful in the dry times when we do not feel Him near, when prayer becomes irksome. You see, God tests our love for Him when prayer seems bothersome. Dry times? They are an opportunity for genuine surrender. Surrender under such conditions promotes spiritual formation."

Brother Lawrence of the Resurrection
The 1st Conversation -
The Practice of the Presence of God

So many wonderful things happened after I promised Mary I would work for her because she saw to my ordination. I was assigned by the Byzantine Eparch to serve as pastor of a little parish I had helped found when still a deacon. At the same time, my own Bishop made me Administrator of a mostly Mexican parish in Queen Creek, Arizona. I was also teaching theology full time in at Seton Catholic High School. I was younger then and loved doing all of it! The Mexican parish had maybe 5% Anglo families of its 400 families, so the English Mass was very small to start, while participation at the Spanish Mass was out the door with people standing outside all the windows. Can you believe the name of the church is Our Lady of Guadalupe!

That cannot be!

After I had been at Our Lady of Guadalupe for a time, Sr. Briege McKenna, a Franciscan nun who ministers to priests was invited to give a retreat in Tucson. The Tucson Diocese invited our Phoenix priests to attend, so I drove down to see what I could learn from this fine nun. The first evening she came to the table where I was sitting and sat right across from me with her dinner tray. After some small talk, she noticed my wedding ring and asked about it. Shocked that I was married, she said, "Oh, this cannot be - not at all." She ate in silence and then left. I felt like I had the plague. I went to my room wondering why I had driven so far, and what there might be for a married man in a retreat that seemed crafted for celibate lives only. I felt nothing against her, and had liked her from the start. It was just that I really didn't fit in.

The next morning Sr. Briege came to breakfast, again sat right across from me and gave me a few Miraculous Medals "for your dear children." Then she said, she had thought it over, and it was fine that I was a married priest - and that was that. I love the Irish! At the end of the retreat she said if anyone wanted to be prayed over, they should wait outside a meeting room and she would take us one at a time. Most went on home, but a handful of us lined up. When it came my turn, I closed the door behind me and took my place on a folding chair - knee to knee with Sister. She took both of my hands, closed her eyes, prayed for me and then began to tell me what she was discerning. I had no idea she had this gift, although later I learned many priests had benefited from it.

She said: "Father, I see the Virgin Mary with a key in her hand - she opens doors for you. I see Ps.91 - You must never be afraid, because God will protect and take care of you." Then she said, "I see the Transfiguration but I don't know what that means." I said nothing, but I now knew exactly what that meant - theosis - the core of my spiritual life. Finally, she said she saw me standing at the foot of the altar with a jug in my hand and people coming down the aisles with cups to be filled. She said the jug contained the teachings that I had to have ready to pour into their cups, because they were thirsty for it. She said I must sit with Jesus and the gospel for the day - every day - and ask him to help me with it - to fill the jug with what can satisfy their thirst. Then she said she saw more and more people coming down the aisles - and finally that they were literally pouring down the aisles. This did not sound like my little church in Queen Creek at all, but I accepted it, thanked her, and went back to Phoenix. That was February of 1992.

Blooming in the Desert

Two months later I received a call from one of the members of the Priest Placement Committee. The Priest Placement Committee advises the Bishop on the decisions he is making about parish openings. I was told the Bishop wanted me at St. Anne parish in Gilbert – and that I must send him a response immediately. At the time, St. Anne's was an eleven hundred family parish in a quiet little town that was just starting to grow. I was there 14 years and saw the parish grow to nearly 9,000 registered families.

Gilbert become the fastest growing town of its size in the entire country! People literally poured down the aisles - even after we built a new church to seat 1200, we were registering over a hundred new families every month. Oh, Sister Briege - they were indeed thirsty! So, my work for Mary had already taken me to a mostly Mexican parish and now to a parish that had only 135 brown faces when I started - but since I pulled out all the stops to make Hispanics welcome, it had grown to be several thousand of Our Lady of Guadalupe's favored children. They call her La Morenita - the little dark one, and of course she has a place of honor in that parish church in Gilbert.

The Mountains of Mexico

While I was their pastor, we were invited to visit some Mexican Indigenous - the Totonaca people in the Sierra mountains inland from Vera Cruz. It was to see if we could find a way to plant the Catechesis of the Good Shepherd in their community. This was suggested at a conference of Catechists being held that year in Assisi. A priest had attended and asked for help there.

We decided to go - working for the Lady again! That is where we met the Missionary Sisters of St. Therese of Lisieux, who had been my saint and mentor even before I was Catholic.

When we arrived at Hueytlalpan, a village of the Totonaca where Carmelite priests were caring for the parish we were told some of its history. These Mesoamerican people were among the first converts to Christianity following the coming of Our Lady of Guadalupe to Tepeyac. Their colonial church was dedicated in the 1550's, just a few years after the 1531 apparitions. That colonial church still serving as their parish church, there had sometimes been priests and sometimes not.

The Diocesan priests who had been serving them about 3 years before we arrived had been driven out by a local Mexican landowner with whom there had been a major confrontation. One catechist was shot and another fled - and the priests took off.

The Bishop had asked the Carmelites to go to Hueytlalpan because none of his own priests really wanted to go. The Carmelites were willing to go for 3 years only, and in a couple of months would be voting in the Provincial Council to leave- their order's work being the care of historic churches in the cities and retreat work. We absorbed all we could of the mission experience and went back to Arizona feeling we could help them a great deal with things that were needed but for which there was no money - like a new parish vehicle and a new roof for the dining room. The biggest concern for me, however, was the Carmelites plan to leave.

We raised about $50,000. with special collections to give them on our next trip. The Provincial heard we were coming and drove out to the mission - a very long trip. His name was Fr. Nicholas and he was wonderful to talk to - and in English! He told us the mission's name is St. Andrew, but for their time there - the three years - they had given it a second name - St. Therese! She is patroness of missions along with St. Francis Xavier, so it really fit - and of course she was a Carmelite.

The Direction of the Saints

Sitting next to Fr. Nicolas at dinner I told him I really felt God wanted the Carmelites to stay - that these Indians deserved to be served by priests who would commit to serve them and not leave. He asked me why I felt that way and I took a photograph out of my pocket to show him. One of our group had been to St. Therese's home in Lisieux, France and had taken a picture of her statue there. She then came with us on our first trip to Hueytlalpan and took a picture of the colorful dancers in the plaza in front of the mission church. She had forgotten to advance the film so the Saint was presiding over the plaza in the photo.

She gave this photo to me and we took it there on the second trip, while providence arranged for the provincial to be there. I showed him the photo, and said "You put the mission under the protection of St. Therese for your three years here, and look, she showed up! You can't just leave these people."

Fr. Nicolas told me that he was a chemical engineer before he became a priest and he realized this was a double exposure, but that it was clear she wanted something from them. He asked what I thought. I told him I felt she wanted them to stay, to commit to these people, and to send some of their best priests to Hueytlalpan, and not just men who were a problem to place. I stressed the need for young priests who could learn the language and culture. He looked at me and said, "Our best?" I said yes, that the Totonaca were as important as the retreatants they were serving and the work they were doing in the historic churches.

A month or so later the Provincial Council of the Carmelites voted to stay at Hueytlalpan. It is more than 20 years now and they are still there, and send all young men who want a Carmelite vocation to the village for a time because it is now an integral part of their work in Mexico. I felt at the time that I was sort of the ugly American, sticking my nose in where it did not belong - but I did it anyway, and I think we are not always comfortable when providence presses us to something, but afterward do feel it was exactly right. In addition to meeting the priests we also met the Missionary Sisters of St. Therese of Lisieux who were working in those mountains in villages near Hueytlalpan for more than 40 years.1550

Chapter 7 – More about Mary & the Saints

"On each fresh occasion of combat, when the enemy desires to challenge me, I conduct myself valiantly: knowing that to fight a duel is an unworthy act, I turn my back upon the adversary without ever looking him in the face; then I run to my Jesus and tell Him I am ready to shed every drop of blood in testimony of my belief that there is a Heaven, I tell Him I am glad to be unable to contemplate, while on earth, with the eyes of the soul, the beautiful Heaven that awaits me so He will deign to open it for eternity to poor unbelievers."

St. Therese of Lisieux
Story of A Soul, Chapter IX

There is so much to say about the Mother of God and the saints! I first met her in my heart long before I ever met her in the Church. In college, I kept thinking about her chapel in St. Paul Cathedral. While years have passed since those college days, the sense of her presence for me in that chapel has not faded. I bought a statue of her and kept it all through college. I did not really have any devotions except the rosary, and since I was not sure how to pray it, I simply held it when I wanted to feel her near. It wasn't really until some years later that I bought my first rosary and a little booklet on how to pray it.

When I was Rector of my Episcopal parish in Minnesota I bought a larger figure of the Holy Mother and kept it in the Rectory. Although I still didn't pray the rosary very often, I was always aware that Mary held some interest in my priesthood. It was when I arrived in Nogales that my Marian devotion really took shape. I was drawn very strongly to Our Lady of Guadalupe's image, and bought one about ten inches high for my office. I had not heard of her until moving to the Southwest.

Then one day a Protestant minister from Nogales, Sonora stopped at our rectory and wanted to talk. I am not sure what his motive may have been since we were a few miles from his side of the border. I thought it may have been economic since he was pastor for a very, very poor church. In any case, he invited me to come with him to see his church and visit one of his families. I did go, and his church was indeed very small and very poor. He took me to visit one of his families , a woman with several small children - very poor. She made thick Mexican coffee for us and gave each of us two saltine crackers. Her children sang a little song for us. On our way back to his church, we passed a house with ceramic tiles of the Virgin of Guadalupe mounted on the wall by the front door. He pointed to it, his face very angry. He said, "That is the whore that keeps Mexico Catholic." I said nothing to him and rode back to the American side of the border in silence.

I tell you this because it perfectly illustrates the contempt in which she is held by some fundamentalists. They neither know her, nor the wonderful gift she is to the Church - to us. I met this hostility again in Arizona after I became Catholic. My one daughter was shown a photo where she worked by a proud mother which showed her son on his mission in Mexico, He was standing in front of a Catholic Church. He had written on the back side of the photo, "Here I am, standing in front of the enemy!" My daughter, who is very direct, told the mother exactly what she thought of that. They, too, did not really know Mary - nor were they able to appreciate who she is for the Universal Church.

True Devotion

Back when I was sure I wanted to convert , I went one day to Picture Rocks Retreat Center near Tucson. I had driven up there several times from Nogales on my days off, because it was such a nice place to pray. (If you haven't picked up on it yet, I am very visual. I think that is why God used visions and dreams with me.) On this visit, I really wanted to talk with a Redemptorist priest, which I had not done before, staying quiet and anonymous. When I arrived and asked about seeing someone, I was told to wait in the library as the priest was with someone else but would be out soon. In the library, I started looking over the books and came upon a shelf with a dozen or so identical little blue hardcover books. Curious, I pulled one and it was St. Louis Marie De Monfort's, "True Devotion to the Blessed Virgin Mary." I started reading it and wow, what a whole new understanding of her began to emerge - just in a few pages.

Fr. Shuster, one of the priests at the center came out and called me into another room. I told him I would like to go to confession, even while knowing that since I was not yet Catholic he could not give me absolution - but could still advise me. Fr. Shuster heard my confession, and while we talked he also was made aware I wanted to convert. When we finished, he did give me absolution, which was a wonderful and welcomed gift.

I told him about the nine days and about my growing relationship with Mary. We also talked about the vision I had experienced in my Episcopal parish just before leaving Minnesota for Arizona - but I did not understand it. I had already met Saint Therese of Lisieux and she was in it, but it was all a mystery to me. He listened intently as I related my vision - I was praying in the church and in my mind I saw a young nun I knew to be St. Therese standing in front of the cross. She was talking to Jesus. Then his right hand left the cross and handed her a bright crystal box. She received it very reverently and then turned to a group of people on her left, handing it to one of them. I did not know who they were, but watched as each one in turn took it and very reverently passed it to the next. Finally, it was given to a man in a cassock, who opened it and turned it upside down - a string of pearls fell from it down toward me. That was it.

Fr. Shuster asked if I realized this was an exact description of intercessory prayer. Of course I did not. He told me that he believed the vision showed that St. Therese prayed to Jesus for the graces I was going to need, and he gave them to her - in the box. It was crystal for purity - the Virgin's purity - because all graces pass to her children through her. The people Therese gave it to were various saints who were praying for me and who would teach me about the spiritual life through their writings. The man in the black cassock he did not identify - patron saint? Maybe St. Ignatius Loyola who is my birth saint? I still don't know who that was. The pearls he said are graces, all strung together.

That was it. I asked him if I could take out the book on True Devotion to Mary and he said yes - and that I should keep it. He advised me to learn all that I could about Mary because she was going to play a very important role in my life. I credit him for making me feel welcome in my future Church, and for his affirmation of the vision and of the nine days which he also validated. He said I was to trust them and walk with God on the path he was pointing out to me. God Bless Fr. Shuster. He has passed now, but is vividly alive in my memory as one of those special people God had in place to help me find my way.

The "Contract"

Another really important encounter with Mary happened in Nogales on March 5, 1979. It was six months before we converted. A parishioner, knowing my love for Mary, brought me a painting of Our Lady. It was very nice and I put it in my office, which was also my prayer room. I hung it on the wall and then knelt to offer my gratitude. When finished, I felt very strongly I should "cut a deal with her." I know that sounds crude, but that is how it came to my mind. There were things I really wanted from her, and there were things I really wanted to promise her as well. I reached for a little notebook and began to write down what amounted to a covenant. This is what I wrote:

MARY'S PART:

1. that she protect me and my family
2. that she guide me
3. that she make me a temple for God
4. that she take me by the hand to Jesus when I die.

MY PART:

1. I will serve God wherever He wants me.
2. I will love and honor her for the rest of my life as my Mother and Queen

I was so sincere - and it felt like a really important thing to be doing at that time. That night I went to bed before Nancy and as soon as I closed my eyes I saw in my mind her hands - holding my notebook and a pen out toward me, and I "heard" an emphatic "Write in your book, AMEN!"

I have something for you

Her protection of our family during those years of transition and vulnerability is really illustrated well by what she did about our housing when we first converted. We were teaching at an inner city school, St. Mark, in a very challenging neighborhood. Our salary was five hundred a month each, with no benefits and only for nine months a year. Our rent in an apartment a block from the school was three hundred fifty a month. We had to feed our four children, pay utilities and any medical bills, buy gas, all on what was left. To make it more stressful for me, the neighborhood woke up at night with loud music, street noise, and occasionally gun shots. I had never lived in a city before, and feared for my family.

One morning before school, while Nancy was getting ready, I went to my icon of Mary in the corner of our small front room and begged her to help me. I had her promise to protect my family, but this was a whole different level of threat for me. When I finished my prayer, I looked up at the icon and I heard a voice, kind but firm, "Don't fret, I have something for you." After that Nancy came down the stairs and we walked over to the school with our son, who was in first grade. When we went through the gate Nancy headed for her room and I stopped in the office to see our Principal. As I entered, the receptionist said, "I have something for you!" I stopped in my tracks and listened. She said her uncle Joe told her it was not very safe for our little children to go outside to play in our neighborhood, and he wanted us to move into a house he owned in Tempe - in a nice safe area.

I called him and told him that we appreciated his offer, but we could not afford to rent a house in Tempe. He asked me, "How much are you paying now? " I told him that we were paying $350, to which he said that happened to be the rent on his house. I learned later that his mortgage payments were twice that amount.

"Uncle Joe" took care of our housing until I got my first parish. It has never been easy for us to take charity from others because we see ourselves as the ones who should always give to others. But this was a time when we did not have a choice, and it taught us so many lessons we would never have learned any other way. God bless Uncle Joe, who had a heart big enough to include everyone.

Suffering a long final illness, he passed away in Christ and I was able to celebrate his funeral Mass.

In sickness and in health

There were so many times in those early days as a Catholic that Mary showed herself to be true to her word. One example from those days was when our youngest son was just an infant after we moved into those neighborhood apartments. He got very, very sick and had to be hospitalized. We were teaching, the girls were in daycare at St. Pius X in Phoenix, our six-year-old was in school with us, and now our little one is in the hospital. The doctors were not optimistic since our son had malabsorption syndrome and they could not identify the virus.

I went to the pastor of our parish and asked him what he thought we should do. He gave me a green scapular of Mary Immaculate and told me to pin it on our son's pillow and ask her help. After school, we hurried to the hospital and I pinned the scapular to his pillow. He looked so terrible we could barely stand it. I told the nurses that if anyone removed that scapular I would own their hospital! They took me seriously and made sure it stayed where it was. Finally, the doctors figured out what virus was causing our son's illness (from Mexican doctors I think, because we had come from the border), and were able to get him better. He had to have predigested formula for many months after that, which was very expensive, but we had our son!

The joy of the restored health of our baby was dampened by the news that his hospital bill was $25,000. We had no insurance at school, no one did. In desperation Nancy called my former treasurer in Nogales to see if they had canceled my health insurance yet. He said it was not canceled yet and the payment to extend it was a hundred dollars. Nancy said we did not have enough money and that blessed man said, "Don't worry Nancy, I'll pay it. He did, and the insurance paid the entire bill. What can I say? Charity chewed up a lot of pride in me, and taught me what we were going to owe others - a debt of love we can never repay.

The picture

Another story I want to share with you of our Mother's love was when I agreed to go to the Gilbert parish. Word got around that I was a married priest and would not fit in. I considered backing out, but instead went to South Phoenix about a week before I was to be at this new assignment. There was a prayer group there under the patronage of Our Lady Of Guadalupe, and they prayed the rosary each week in the family's back yard. I went and sat in the shadows under a tree so I would not be approached by anyone, as some attending knew me - and I very much wanted to be alone. I prayed, begging our Lady to come with me to the new assignment, as I wasn't wanted there and I did not know what this would mean for my family.

After the prayers, I left as folks were chatting with each other - and as I reached the way out of the backyard a woman called out to me - "Father Doug, I have something for you!" Those words again! I went back and the woman took a photograph out of her purse. She said she had come to a talk I had given on Mary a year ago, that she had taken my picture while I was speaking at the ambo, and that she then went to a Marian conference in California and took a picture of a beautiful statue of Mary they had at the conference. When they developed the roll of film, three other pictures were on the negatives between the one she took of me and the one she took of Mary in California. Somehow, they were in one negative - the Mary negative. There she was, in perfect proportion, watching over me.

The woman whose back yard we were praying in looked at the picture and said to me, "You must never be afraid because she goes everywhere with you." She had no idea I had a new assignment and that I was fearing what I would meet there. I was numb, really, but felt I would now be alright. In addition, she had the photo in her purse nearly a year...and it ends up in my hands exactly when I needed it.

Sometime later, I asked for the roll of negatives and took them to a film expert in Scottsdale, Arizona. He kept them for a week and when I picked them up he said there were several other negatives between the one of Mary and the one of me, and that getting them together on one negative was just impossible unless maybe light had hit the lens in such a way with the second photo that it refracted somehow and planted the one image on the other. He said I should consider it a totally unexplainable photo and was a double exposure that was way more than a simple double exposure. I often think St. Therese called on her sister, Celene, who was the convent photographer who took all of the photos of Therese!

Clothed in protection

Armed with that picture, I went a week later to my new assignment, met a lot of resistance, but eventually stayed fourteen years, built the new church, established many lay ministries in two languages, and all relying on Our Lady. It cost me dearly, and was way beyond my capabilities because it required a lot of administration - something for which I was not well prepared. Managing the eleven hundred family parish I entered was fine. But when it exploded into thousands of families, I just struggled my way through it all. But, the spiritual development of the parish, and its many lay ministries flourished and flowered and was so fruitful that they still talk about those days.

The Spiritual warfare at St. Anne was, however relentless. For me, it was like when the Israelites returned from captivity to rebuild Jerusalem and had to rebuild the walls and temple with a tool in one hand and a weapon in the other. We learned why on April 20th - Hitler's birthday. A tent appeared on the grass at the back of the property where there were still pecan trees from the former pecan Grove that St. Anne's bought for our new church. Three or four young men were there and had made a small circular stone altar, and had black candles they planned to use to worship Satan. They said they came every year on April 20th as the Grove had been dedicated to him. Now we knew, and prayed special prayers over the property to help blunt the enemy's influence. The cult returned each year and were sent away by our Knights of Columbus who patrolled the property each April 20th. Satan does not give up his temples easily, and it took repeated prayers right up to the time I left that assignment.

Some assignments are like that. Sometimes we are asked, in our priestly life, to do things that will cost us, but will produce wonderful fruit that will last. That was very much the case with our fourteen years in Gilbert. Mary helps us do what is beyond us, and maybe that is also good because we can't take credit for how everything came out in the end - there is less chance for pride to gnaw away at our hearts - which is exactly what it does.

Remember Sister Briege? What Jesus wanted was a spiritual house at the Gilbert parish - and I did as Sister said and sat with Jesus every single day to prepare my homily and teachings. I have done that faithfully for 25 years now. If he had wanted a fine administrator there, to manage the unforeseen population growth, he would have moved the Bishop to send them one. We had some priests with real talent in administration. The trick is to first find out what heaven wants, and then arrange everything we can to make it happen. For me, it is always the Lady who knows what God wants....and she goes with me, which makes it all not always easy, but do-able.

When I was thinking about converting with my family, I was still Rector in Nogales. I was struggling as a childhood evangelical with how important Mary is with the Catholics and the Orthodox.

Was it really honoring God and the role he assigned to her in our salvation, or was it, as my German Lutheran upbringing would say, dishonoring him. So I asked the Holy Spirit to teach me something that would make it easier to understand.

The Lady of the House

I closed my eyes and in my imagination, I saw a great mansion, with a back door. There were street urchins, such as the homeless, unwashed kids we see in some English literary classics. Mary, dressed as a kitchen maid with apron came out the door and invited the children to come in, and some did. They were seated at the servants table in the kitchen area, and served food. It was a mess because they stuffed rolls in their pockets, didn't use the napkin, ate with their fingers.... you get the idea. But Mary gently taught them, day by day when they would show up to eat, and in time some of them were really civilized! When they reached a certain level, she would scrub them, put them in a nice set of clothes, and take them into the main part of the mansion to a great staircase. I realized it lead to the Master of the house and his great room. She would take them by the hand and lead them up the steps, introduced them to the Master (who knew they were there all along), and tell him they were ready to come and live in his fine house.

As spouse of the Holy Spirit, she works for him, and as mother of humanity - the new Eve, she mothers her children spiritually. This story settled my heart, and I knew what she was doing not only honored God, but helped Jesus receive the reward of his suffering - US! If we stay in her kitchen, she will take us by the hand to Jesus, and it will be our turn to receive the reward of his suffering - HIM! And through him, the Father, and the Holy Spirit. Theosis!

One last note: When our youngest son nearly died of mal-absorption syndrome from a virus they had such a time identifying, he recovered, but developed childhood asthma and was having a terrible time breathing. I think he was less than a year old, and I had used up my 5 sick days staying home with him. I was worried sick, and just held him most of the time. On the 5th day home from teaching, I stood in front of the Icon of Mary that let me know she had something for me (Uncle Joe's house) and told her she had to do something to help him. Of course, I cried. I love my family and without them I would certainly not have been able to be a priest - I would have died of a great loneliness. That evening his breathing was normal, and he has never had asthma again. That Icon is in our oldest twin daughter's home now, but I love it still, because it made Mary very present to me in those difficult times.

Chapter 8 – The Sisters

"On each fresh occasion of combat, when the enemy desires to challenge me, I conduct myself valiantly: knowing that to fight a duel is an unworthy act, I turn my back upon the adversary without ever looking him in the face; then I run to my Jesus and tell Him I am ready to shed every drop of blood in testimony of my belief that there is a Heaven, I tell Him I am glad to be unable to contemplate, while on earth, with the eyes of the soul, the beautiful Heaven that awaits me so He will deign to open it for eternity to poor unbelievers."

St. Therese of Lisieux
Story of A Soul, Chapter IX

We had raised money at St. Anne to send three of the Totonaca women catechists to Rome to study the Catechesis of the Good Shepherd under one of the the founders, Sophia Cavaletti. We wanted to introduce the Catechesis to the parish in Hueytlalpan. Of the three that we raised funds for, only one of the women could go. She was the wife of the catechist who had been shot to death. But now her oldest son who was acting as the male head of the family said no.

What to do? We had funds to send three, but now had no one to send. Fr. Carlos Martinez, our blessed guide in all of this (together with Maria Cristlieb, a catechist from Mexico City) suggested we send three of the Carmelite Sisters. So we did. One was Mexican and the other two Indigenous Mexicans. No one ever sent Indigenous off to study so far away, fearing culture shock. The culture shock never happened! While in Rome they lived with the Sacred Heart Sisters as their guests. After their months with Sophia in Rome, we sent them to Lisieux to visit their Patroness, St.Therese. When they returned to Mexico one of the indigenous Sisters wrote me a letter, with a wonderful insight - she said she realized now that she could be a Sister anywhere!

The Sisters had been working for many years in those mountain villages, but we did not meet them until Fr. Carlos introduced them as good substitutes for the women we had wanted to send to Rome from Hueytlalpan. We stayed very connected to the Sisters after that, with trips to the Mother House in Puebla with busloads of pilgrims. We met Sr. Socorro early on, and since she spoke a little English we all gravitated to her.

Sometime later, Sr. Socorro called me from Merced, California - to greet me. She said she was there selling cookies and cakes and brown scapulars to raise money for the order. I invited her to Arizona, and over time that invitation lead to St. Anne's hiring several of the Sisters to work in the parish. Now, so many years later, they are established here and work in three different parishes. What a blessing they have been for us, and for the large Hispanic population of devout Catholics who live here.

The Convent in the Mountains

As I said, our parish would regularly travel to the Mother House in Puebla, Mexico as an expression of our support and affection for the Missionary Sisters of St. Therese of Lisieux. On one of these parish pilgrimages to the Mother House of the order, we were taken to visit their "convent" in Ixtepec. For decades, they had worked there with the Indigenous who populated the town, living in what would never pass an inspection in the States. I decided then and there my parish would do all it could to help these Sisters. We would do special collections to help them build a proper convent. After all, if we were having a nice new church, shouldn't we try to help them ?

The spirit and generosity or our parishioners was evident when they offered nearly a $100,000 in four collections and gave it all to the Sisters - no strings attached! The sisters were able to build the most beautiful Convent for those mountains in Ixtepec, Mexico. The convent can house thirty nuns, serves as a conference center for religious of any number of different orders working in the Sierra's, and looks like a big white dove on the hillside. It has private room for guests, a large dormitory for many sisters, a beautiful chapel, a nice kitchen and dining room, and a large cistern for rain water - everything!

The Sisters invited us to Ixtepec for the dedication of the new convent - a whole group of us went. Sitting by the entrance in a little sitting area, we watched a Totonaca man walk up the street stairs and knock on the door. A Sister answered, and as he talked to her, her eyes filled with tears. Just as quickly as he had come, he left. We asked her what he had said to her. She told us he had come to tell her that he and the other locals had come to believe the Sisters were not staying. (40 years they had been there!) But now that they had built their big white house, he knew they would never leave! In addition to Ixtepec, part of the collections went toward a beautiful Convent in Amazoc.

The Porter's Rope

Some time later when John Paul II came to Mexico City to canonize Juan Diego - the first Indigenous saint for Mexico - the Sisters called and told me they had gotten a ticket for me! Of course, we went - a deacon from Gilbert went down with me even though there was only one ticket. God bless him. My seat was just outside the giant doors of her Temple, in a blazing July sun, but I didn't care - I was there! And to make it all better, it was my birthday - July 31, 2002.

Juan Diego worked for Our Lady in such a humble way, launching an evangelization that saw 8 million Indigenous baptized - camping out in towns by the thousands, all wanting to be baptized. His humility is what has always impressed me. He said of himself, "I am only a porter's rope." A porter's rope is a piece of rope swung over a load someone is trying to carry on their back. When I think of that I think of the movie, Kung Fu Panda, and the scene where his enemy laughs at him and tells him he is nothing but a big fat panda. He fires back that actually he is THE big fat panda! St. Juan Diego wasn't just a porter's rope - he was HER porter's rope. And that made all the difference.

We can see the great virtues of the saints and wish with all our hearts to be like them, because they have to a great extent recovered by grace the likeness of God. We are all created in his Image, but as we leave childhood behind with words like "Mine!", and "No!", the likeness fades fast. And while we never hope to reach the degree of likeness to God their souls show us, we can cooperate with the graces God gives us, and little by little, walking with him, we can make headway.

St. Therese tells of her mother placing her at the bottom of a steep set of stairs in their house in Alencon. Then mom went to the top and called her to follow. Therese could not even get her knee up on the first step - but she kept trying and trying harder. Finally, mom came down, picked her up, and took her to where she wanted to be. Therese says that mirrors our struggle with choking the passions and practicing the virtues - we only struggle because of the grace we are given to desire the virtue in the first place - and we keep up the struggle against our passions our whole life. She says that at our death we have only made it up a little way, but Jesus picks us up and takes us to where we longed to be - up at the top of the stairs with him. The secret is to keep trying - no matter what.

Gentle and Humble of Heart

Theosis is for us after we die. For a rare few, it happens near the end of their lives here in this world - as a witness to the truth of this ancient way. In every generation, these witnesses are raised up by the Holy Spirit. They, more than anyone else, know the great gulf that exists between two truths - the truth about the Image of God in which we are created, and the sad and tattered remnants of what we see is our own dim likeness to that Image. It is this realization that produces true humility in our hearts - and blesses us. Jesus set me on this path many years ago, and I am ashamed to say I have made very little progress in all the intervening years. That is why I hesitated to write all of this down. If pride is my, our great sickness, won't writing our story just make things worse?

I remember exactly how God put humility right in front of me - as the most important thing Jesus wanted to teach me as I tried to grow up spiritually. This happened back in my Minnesota parish. I had been tormented by the thought that God had something he was waiting for me to do, and I was being totally obtuse. It got to the point where I could not pray. Finally, in frustration, I told him I could not fix this if I didn't know what it was to begin with. I pleaded ignorance and told him he had to make it really clear to me or I wouldn't get it.

This was before the nine days. I got up and walked over to a Bible, intending to read a bit, and opened it. It opened to Matthew 18, and my eyes fell on the words "Learn from me, for I am gentle and humble of heart." I was just staring at the words for a long time. This was it - the very opposite of pride. Then I went to another Bible and opened that - Matthew 18 again. An accident? When I walked over to the church there was a Bible in the sacristy so I played Bible Roulette - which I never do - and again it opened to Matthew 18. I guess God heard me and didn't want me to make a mistake here!

Well, that evening I wanted to read, and had a new book on the sayings of St. Seraphim of Sarov, a popular Russian saint. It had interested me in an ad I had read, so I ordered it without knowing anything about him. Not having read it yet, I sat down and opened it. The page I opened to had the title, "Advice to a young novice." So I read it. The young man asks the saint to teach him how to be a monk. Seraphim answered that only Jesus could do that, and suggested he build a hut and then study the words of Matthew 18 where it says, "Learn from me for I am gentle and humble of heart." Can you believe it? So, if I want to please God, it all starts here - with Jesus words, because the mother of all sin is pride, and the mother of all Godly virtue is humility.

Therese teaches exactly the same truth. It was so strongly believed by her that when she was dying she asked Mother Gonzage - that old aristocrat the nuns said treated her cat better than she treated them - "Mother, do you think I am humble?" Mother Gonzage answered very tenderly, "Yes, my child, I believe you are humble." Of course, it was this sever old nun who formed her in that model. Seraphim is called the St. Therese of the East - both extremely popular in their countries. They lived 70 years apart, but share January 2 - Therese was born on that date, and Seraphim died on that date, 70 years earlier. Both were truly humble.

The one who gives this testimony says, "Yes, I am coming soon." Amen! Come, Lord Jesus! The grace of the Lord Jesus be with all.

Revelation 22:20-12

Chapter 9 – Family is Everything

"If it is displeasing to you to serve the LORD, choose today whom you will serve, the gods your ancestors served beyond the River or the gods of the Amorites in whose country you are dwelling. As for me and my household, we will serve the LORD."."

Joshua 24:14-15

Looking back, I cannot help but see the central place family has taken in my life. But when we were first married, the only real theological notion I had was the scripture - "As for me and my household, we will serve he Lord." Of course, everything goes back to the Trinity, who are the model of family at every level for us. The mutual love and respect that exists between the three divine persons of the Trinity is certainly reflected in Rublev's icon of the three angels visiting Abraham and Sarah by the oak tree at Mamre. This God of ours, who is Himself a family, is reflected in His creation - and most especially, but not exclusively in humankind.

This divine mark of mutual love and respect was present in an ecumenical prayer group that met at my Minnesota parish every week. When Nancy and I left for Arizona they met to pray over us, asking God to keep us safe and bless our future work. Wendell, one of the evangelical members, came to me afterward and said during the prayers he saw me with a saw, cutting wood, and also saw me up in the air with a big cross. A man of very strong faith and really sincere, I thanked him for his words, but in my heart, I thought it was just his love and zeal for Christ, and then I forgot all about it.

Well, he was right! Do you remember the cut - outs of "this is my commandment, that you love one another" I made using a sabre saw? When Wendell said he saw me cutting wood I naturally assumed it was with a regular saw. It dawned on me a few days after I made them and was putting them up.

Me with a big cross in the air? Again, not until I was actually up in the air with a big cross did it dawn on me. St. Andrew had no cross on it to identify it as a church. One day a welder stopped in to see if I needed any metal cattle fences repaired. We didn't have any but in that moment, I thought of our crossless church and asked if he could make me a big aluminum cross. He said yes, and came back with the rectangular tubing to weld it in our carport.

To get it up on the tower, about three stories I think, I put a ladder on the roof, leaning against the tower and barely reaching the wood beams connecting the tower's two parts. There I am, an electric drill and two long U-shaped bolts fastened to my belt, trying to manage this big unwieldy cross in a good wind. I lashed myself to the beams with rope so if I fell I would not drop so far. Nancy is on the ground thinking I am out of my mind and praying I wouldn't fall. We got it up, and later a parishioner grounded it with copper wire. When I finished fastening it into place I remembered Wendell. God was surely telling me through Wendell and that prayer group that there was a plan. Without the mutual love and respect we had in that group, I would have missed a great blessing.

This mutual love and respect, seen so clearly in the Blessed Trinity, extends beyond the grave for us. That is why we pray for the dead. Family is different there, but still family - love never ends! At St. Anne there was a deacon and his beautiful family. His wife was a catechist in our Atria (Catechesis of the Good Shepherd). Devout, the family never missed Mass. The flu struck and moved from one to another and soon hit Daniel who was nearly 9 years old. He woke up with it and was taken to the hospital because it was so severe. In the evening around 6 o'clock he died. Nothing stings the heart like the death of a child, so the family was in deep pain. The next evening, I popped something in the microwave because Nancy was away for a few days. I turned on the 6pm news and a moment later I knew Daniel was standing to the right of the tv, wanting something. But then he was gone. The next evening at 6pm the same thing happened but I sensed him there a little longer. The following day was the funeral Mass. I entered the church from one door at the same time the family entered another. Daniel's mom rushed over to me and excitedly told me that at 6pm the next day after his death, Daniel stood right in front of her as she prepared dinner for the family. (I Had told absolutely no one of my own experince.) I asked her if she

could see him and she said no, but added, "But I know my son." I asked if he said what he wanted and she said he wanted permission to leave! The rule was no one left the house without telling mom where they were going. I asked her what she told him and she said, "I said no." Then she said the whole scene was repeated the next evening, but this time she said yes. Daniel had a place to go, and wanted to go. Then I told her of my experience. Of course there were some tears. If our family love can be so deep, we who are created in his image, what must he himself be like?

This divine mutual love and respect extends also to the great family of the natural world and it's creatures. I never liked snakes - except maybe garter snakes when I was a kid. One day when Nancy and I came back to the rectory there was a big rattlesnake on the floor of our garage. I immediately felt compassion for it, "sensing" it was afraid and in trouble. I can assure you that I NEVER would ever feel anything for a snake. But there I was, trying to sweep it out of the garage with a broom! I even individualized it the next morning with a name, like a pet - Harold I called him. As I kept my distance with the broom he finally went out of the garage to some shrubs near our front door. The next morning I went out there calling him like a puppy, but no Harold, and feeling this unexplainable compassion. Later that morning one of our daughters, carrying her little boy, walked under the thick catclaw trellis leading to the front door and Harold drops down from the catclaw right in front of her! She retreated to her car and called animal control, who took him away telling her he was dehydrated and probably starving. God was wanting me to see how far perfect love extends, because a few days later this infusion of compassion for a serpent was made very clear.

I had stopped at our Catholic bookstore and saw a Cistercian Study Series book - the one I quoted from earlier about St. Isaac the Syrian. I opened it and this is what I read: "And what is a merciful heart? It is the heart burning for all creation, for men, for birds, for animals, for demons, and for every created thing, and by the recollection of them (I think he means seeing what they suffer.) the eyes of a merciful man pour forth abundant tears. By the strong and vehement mercy that grips his heart and by his great compassion, his heart is humbled and he cannot bear to see or hear any injury or slight sorrow in creation. For this reason he offers up tearful prayer continually even for irrational beasts, for the enemies of the truth, and for those who harm him, that they be protected and receive mercy. AND IN LIKE MANNER HE EVEN PRAYS FOR THE FAMILY OF REPTILES because of the great compassion that burns without measure in his heart IN THE LIKENESS OF GOD."

Perfect love for our great family of creation is part of the love and respect we are to pray for. God certainly put his point across to a priest who felt he really loved animals and nature. Well, I did, but not nearly enough.

Parishes are families as well, and mutual love and respect are also their ideal as a community. The parishes I served responded to this imperative in different degrees, each having different histories and composition.

My first assignment after ordination to the priesthood was Our Lady of Guadalupe in Queen Creek, Arizona. What a joy that mission was for me. Two cultures under the same roof, getting along but still separated in so many respects. A wonderful Mexican woman named Maria came up with the idea of serving a breakfast in the hall between the English and Spanish Masses. It worked - food brings people together! Mexicans came early for their Mass and English speakers stayed after their Mass. At first it was a little uncomfortable - like the first meal together for a blended family. Soon some were trying to communicate by gestures, our languages being different. In time some friendships developed - mutual friendships and respect. Love even began to grow between folks who came regularly - crossing cultural lines that once seemed too much to negotiate. A great memory for me now, having seen them trying to be a real family - like God - even if just a pale reflection.

Much is given, much is required

Not long after I was assigned to Our Lady of Guadalupe, the Byzantine Catholic Eparch named me pastor of St. Thomas Byzantine Catholic Church. Since I was already chaplain and theology teacher at Seton Catholic High School, I now had three assignments - plus a family. I had served St. Thomas as a bi-ritual deacon when we were celebrating Divine Liturgy in a little tack room on horse property. It was a nice little "church" but only sat twenty or so people. The Eparchy sold the farm (we were living in the house that was there) and we had Divine Liturgy in the living room of one of the parishioners. After that I got permission to celebrate in the chapel at Seton High School, so we had a larger space. Finally, we bought the old St. Anne church and that is where the little community could feel it was finally home. Our Byzantine Eparch called St. Thomas "a floating crap game"! It was, but our "travels" made us a real family - love and respect - reflecting the Trinity.

I had to give up St. Thomas when I was assigned at St. Anne because St. Anne was starting to feel the effects of Gilbert's building boom and population explosion. They had a handful of Hispanics but the demographic for the parish included some five thousand. At that time, St. Anne parish covered twelve square miles! They certainly were not at St. Anne. So, I opened the doors wide to them, and they came in large numbers - from all over. There was real resistance from the parishioners, and it was clear I had made a very unpopular decision. The German side of my German/Irish ancestry kicked in, and I forged ahead. Since the Church in Arizona was headed toward an eventual Hispanic majority it made no sense at all to limit ministry in Spanish - sending so many to protestant churches who were courting them.

In time, we had over three thousand Hispanic families registered at St. Anne, and six thousand families in the English-speaking community. Wonderful love and respect that reflected the Trinity did develop within the two separate communities for many people, and some real bonding between Hispanics and "Anglos" but apart from these they never really mixed well. Just the large numbers and a very different demographic were reason enough. We offered sacramental preparation in both languages, and scores of ministries, so a strong foundation was laid for the future.

The last chapter

Finally, after fourteen years at St. Anne, I went to St. Maria Goretti in Scottsdale. Wounded multiple times over the years, of the Cross. Authentic or not, God used it in a marvelous way. I had taken it into the chapel for veneration and had knelt to pray. After a few minutes I began to see Mary, sitting on the ground in front of Jesus on his cross. I didn't see him but knew he was there, suffering. She turned to me and reached out her hand, inviting me to take it and join her. I broke into sobs, from my deep heart, and could not stop. Finally, I got up to find some tissue so I could blow my nose and get control of myself. I kept thinking about how she looked. Her face wasn't twisted in pain, but rather stunned at what they had done to him - in shock that one so precious and loving would ever be treated this way. Her heart, to be sure, was being pierced - martyred - in a way too deep for words.

The other thing I kept thinking was how she reached out to me as she would family - to sit with her and be there with her. To console her. Like a son. That is what made me cry so hard. Do you remember Jesus saying anyone who keeps his commandments is his mother and his brother - his own kin? So being an adopted son of the Father is not just a nice sentiment, but is a reality. When St. John of the Cross said that in a moment of theosis God treated him like an equal - like family - it wasn't just a nice sentiment but a very solid reality.

This event carried with it a recognition that Jesus had put me with his mother, and her with me - as family. She really IS our mother. And of course all of this happens because God's defining core is love. When St.Therese was near to dying her sisters gathered around her and asked for her last word. She looked at them and said, LOVE IS EVERYTHING.

If I had one wish at the end of my life, it would be to see our sad world reach the point described by Tielhard de Chardin:

> *"Someday, after mastering the winds, the waves, the tides and gravity, we shall harness for God the energies of love and then, for a second time in the history of the world, man will have discovered fire."*

(Fr. Doug's website is frdouginherhands.com)

Afterword: Faith's Journey

Dan Hahne

If the depth of a soul's spirituality is measured by its capacity to serve through love, then Fr. Doug Lorig is a profoundly spiritual man. Growing up in a small Midwestern town, Father knew his role within creation's expansive drama was set upon a universal stage. Moved by a personal nature inclined to compassionate self-giving, Father embraced a life of service. As a social worker, minister, priest and pastor, and as a loving father and husband to his wife and soulmate Nancy, he was led by his belief in the sublime goodness of creation, a creation freely given by a magnanimous and benevolent God who seeks communion with each soul. Forged by this inspired vision, Father's life became a bridge that traversed the often misunderstood divide between our material and spiritual natures culminating, through the urging of our Blessed Mother, in his acceptance of a profound calling to be a Catholic priest as a married family man.

Rooted in common experience and faith, Father Doug's life and words offer an expanded vision of what it means to live Christ's word. It is a message driven by the heart and guided by the mind. A message that aspires to have us see the good in creation and our neighbor and to seek the advancement of peaceful coexistence with our global brothers and sisters. Whether through merciful giving, conversations over coffee or through homiletics, Father communicated his unique understanding that God's call to love is man's call to love through action. As expressed by the Jesuit priest and visionary, Fr. Pierre Teilhard de Chardin (a scientist and theologian whose life and work Father greatly regards) it is through loving, by being an agent of good in the world, that each soul advances the human condition in its participation in and ascent of The Divine Milieu. Father's insightful autobiography is an inspiration that portrays a life devoted to the Gospel and a vision that perceives the everyday not as an impediment, but as a gateway to our ultimate fulfillment, a fulfillment that rests upon the cornerstones of our Divine Father's two greatest commandments, "Thou shalt love the Lord thy God with thy whole heart and with thy whole soul and with thy whole mind" and "thou shalt love thy neighbor as thyself."

www.ingramcontent.com/pod-product-compliance
Lightning Source LLC
Chambersburg PA
CBHW031413040426
42444CB00005B/541
* 9 7 8 0 9 8 3 3 2 5 7 1 0 *